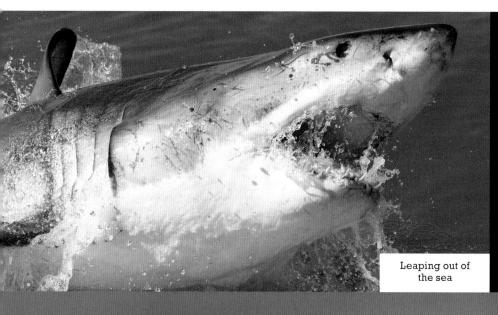

Athletic hunter

Great white sharks hunt for large prey, such as sea lions, seals and small toothed whales. To catch prey like seals the shark swims very quickly to the surface of the water before leaping out and grabbing the seal in its powerful jaws. The shark will then drag the seal below the surface to be eaten.

Leaping out of the sea

Factfile

More predatory sharks

Sharks are successful and efficient hunters. Over millions of years their bodies have evolved into killing machines.

Tiger shark

Tiger sharks have been nicknamed the dustbins of the sea due to their reputation for eating anything in their path.

Bull shark

The aggressive bull shark has a diet of bony fish and other sharks. These vicious predators will even eat other bull sharks.

Sharks have strong muscular bodies

Designed to kill

Great whites are the largest predatory fish on Earth, and their bodies are made for killing. They have a skeleton made of cartilage, which is flexible and lightweight, making this killing machine fast and strong.

Keen senses

Sharks use their acute senses of smell, sight, and touch to hunt. They have nerve-packed strips, called lateral lines, that run down the sides of their bodies, which detect the faint vibrations of living things in water. Great white sharks can sense even tiny amounts of blood in the water from 5 km away. They are also able to smell a colony of seals from over 3 km away.

A great white shark bites into a tuna

Blacktip shark

The blacktip shark's diet is made up of sardines, herring, catfish and mackerel. They will also eat rays and skates.

African lion

African lions are the second **largest** of all the big cats (tigers are slightly bigger). They live in the **savannahs** and plains of the south **Sahara** Desert and in parts of southern and eastern Africa, where their tan-coloured coats provide perfect **camouflage** for **hunting** during sunset. Lions live in large groups called prides. The members of the **pride** work together to hunt animals far bigger than themselves. Lions will stalk and attack **wildebeest**, zebra, giraffe and even **rhinoceroses** and hippopotamuses. Male lions are the only members of the cat family to have **manes**.

Facts and figures

Scientific name Panthera leo	**Group name** Pride
Type Mammal	**Habitat** Savannah grassland
Size Head to tail from 2.1 to 3 metres	**Range** Most of sub-Saharan Africa
Weight Up to 190 kg	**Diet** From small hares and reptiles to wildebeest, impala, zebra and large buffalos
Life span in the wild Up to 18 years	
Running speed Up to 58 km per hour	**Meal size** Up to 27 kg

A male African lion showing his strong teeth

A lion's roar is so loud it can be heard from 8 kilometres away!

Lions' land

Each lion pride has a specific area that it controls. This territory can be as large as 260 square kilometres of scrub, grasslands or open woodland.

Defence duty

Male lions leave a scent on trees and bushes as a warning to other animals that they are trespassing on the pride's territory.

Did you know?

Asian lions are smaller than their African relatives. They once roamed from the Middle East to India, but now there are less than 260 Asian lions surviving in the wild.

Male lion attacking a huge buffalo bull

More African cats

Among the many beautiful animals that are native to Africa are some of the most ferocious and deadly predators on Earth.

Cheetah
Cheetahs are the fastest land mammal. They can run at 96 km per hour. They will hunt for hares, gazelles and impala.

Leopard
Leopards hunt antelope, deer and pigs. They are strong climbers who often drag their prey up into trees to be eaten.

Caracal
The caracal is a fierce wild cat. It hunts small animals, such as mice, springhares and birds, but is also able to kill larger animals.

A lioness hunting a young zebra

Super predator

Lions work together when they hunt and usually catch their victims by sneaking up on them as closely as possible before suddenly launching an attack. A lion will wrestle the animal to the ground and then strangle or suffocate it by clamping down on its neck.

Female hunters

Female lions are the main hunters in the pride they do 85 to 90 per cent of the hunting. When they have killed their prey they allow the male lions to be the first to eat. The lionesses will eat next and the lion cubs will eat whatever meat is left. Fighting over food is common in a pride of lions.

Lion eyes

The lion's eyesight is no better than a human's during the day, but in the dark of night the lion is able to see eight times better. A lion's eye is able to enhance even the faintest light given off by the stars and the moon. Lions make the most of this excellent night vision by doing the majority of their hunting in the dark.

Lions have very good night vision

Crocodile

The crocodile's reputation for being an **aggressive** and dangerous predator is entirely justified. These huge **reptiles** are known to **attack** anything that crosses their path – including humans! Crocodiles have the most **powerful** bite of any creature on Earth. Once prey has been caught in these long **massive** jaws, there is no **escape**. Even large animals, such as buffalo and **wildebeest**, can be killed and eaten by these huge reptiles; the crocodile simply drags its prey **underwater** and holds it there until it has **drowned**.

Facts and figures

Scientific name Crocodylidae	**Group name** Bask (on land) or float (in water)
Type Reptile	**Habitat** Wetlands, lakes, rivers and coastal areas
Size Body length from 1.5 to 5.2 metres	**Range** Africa, the Americas, Australia and Asia
Weight Up to 900 kg	**Diet** Fish, turtles and many other larger animals
Life span in the wild Up to 70 years	
Swimming speed Up to 40 km per hour	**Meal size** Up to 115 kg

Keeping cool

Crocodiles don't have sweat glands and so release heat through their mouths. They often sleep with their mouths wide open and may even pant like a dog!

Giant crocodile

The saltwater crocodile, also known as the estuarine or Indo-Pacific crocodile, is the largest of all living reptiles.

Did you know?

Crocodiles have good vision during the day. They use their sight to help them catch prey on land. Underwater the crocodile's sight is impaired and so it uses other senses to hunt.

A Nile crocodile resting on a log to keep cool

A crocodile lying in wait in the water

Waiting patiently

Crocodiles are ambush predators. A crocodile will lie under the water's surface and wait very patiently for an animal to come to the water to drink and, when one does, the crocodile will quickly jump up to grab the unsuspecting animal. The crocodile then drags the prey underneath the water to be drowned.

Keeping warm

Cold-blooded crocodiles rely on external heat to warm up their bodies. This is why they spend hours basking on river banks and shorelines in the hot tropical sunshine. They will move into areas with cooler air or water temperatures if they get too hot.

Nile crocodiles have been known to live for up to 100 years (in captivity)!

Enormous appetite

Crocodiles can have ferocious appetites. It is known for a Nile crocodile to eat up to half its body weight at a feeding. Nile crocodiles mainly eat fish, but will attack almost anything that crosses their path. Larger prey includes porcupines, birds, small hippopotamuses, zebras, and even other crocodiles.

A Nile crocodile with its catch

Stone power

Stones are often found in the stomachs of crocodiles. It is believed the stones may help digestion.

Thick skinned

The skin covering the crocodile's back is covered in bony plates. It is so thick it can deflect arrows, spears and even bullets!

Attacking wildebeest

Golden eagle

The **magnificent** golden eagle is a large bird of prey with broad wings and a longish tail. These **stunning** birds are usually solitary or live in pairs. They are most often seen **soaring** or **gliding** with their wings lifted into a slight 'V' shape. Golden eagle pairs maintain **territories** as large as 155 square kilometres. They use their **massive** sharp talons for hunting and defence. They mostly hunt **medium-sized** animals, such as hares, **rabbits**, squirrels, young foxes and rodents. They will also sometimes eat smaller birds, **insects**, snakes and fish.

Facts and figures

Scientific name Aquila chrysaetos	**Group name** Convocation
Type Bird	**Habitat** Shrublands, forests, and grasslands
Size Wingspan from 1.8 to 2.3 metres	**Range** North America, Asia, Africa and Europe
Weight Up to 7 kg	**Diet** Rabbits, hares, birds squirrels, reptiles, fish and insects
Life span in the wild Up to 30 years	
Flying speed Up to 50 km per hour	**Meal size** Up to 4 kg

Golden eagles often compete with **wolves** for the same **prey**.

Acute eyesight

Unlike most birds, the eyes of the golden eagle both point forward. This enables them to judge distances with great accuracy and is an essential tool when hunting.

An adult golden eagle in the attack position

Shell-shocked

Some golden eagles eat tortoises. They hold the tortoise in their talons and then drop it on to a rock to break the shell open.

Did you know?

The feathers of a golden eagle are, in fact, brown. This large bird of prey gets its name because sunlight shining on the feathers reflects a shimmering golden colour.

Double attack

Two golden eagles will often hunt together. They will glide at low levels until they spot prey, then one eagle will chase it until it starts to show signs of exhaustion. At this point the other eagle takes over and will suddenly dive down to seize the animal with its powerful curved talons.

Deadly talons

A golden eagle's feet are kitted out with four dagger-like talons. Each talon can be over 5 centimetres long. These sharp claws are used for grabbing prey and are strong enough to pierce skin. The eagle has a special locking mechinism in its legs that prevents its grip from slipping.

A golden eagle swooping down

A golden eagle eating its prey

The eagle's beak is a powerful tool

Knife-like beak

The beak of the golden eagle is specially adapted for the type of food that it eats. There is a hook at the front that can cut into meat like a knife, while the sides of the beak have razor-sharp edges to tear flesh from prey. In fact, a hungry eagle can strip all the flesh from a rabbit in just 15 minutes.

Rattlesnake

There are over 30 different **rattlesnake** species. Each has a **vibrating** rattle at the end of its tail, which acts as a warning to stay clear of these scaly **predators**. Their large fangs can inject a **venom** that stuns and even kills. They live in North and South America, and can be found in most **habitats**, including **mountains**, deserts and plains. Rattlesnakes survive on a diet of small mammals, such as **mice**, rats, small birds and other rodents. Generally their prey is **bitten** once and then released. The venom quickly kills the prey and then the snake **swallows** it whole.

Facts and figures

Scientific name Crotalus	**Group name** Rhumba
Type Reptile	**Habitat** Sandy woodlands and coastal scrub
Size Body length from 0.6 to 2.4 metres	**Range** North and South America
Weight Up to 15.4 kg	
Lifespan in the wild Up to 20 years	**Diet** Rodents, squirrels, rabbits and other small animals
Average speed Up to 6 km per hour	**Meal size** up to 2.5 kg

An Arizona blacktail rattlesnake sensing with its forked tongue

Some **rattlesnakes hibernate** in the **cold winter** months inside **underground dens.**

Did you know?

The rattlesnake has two sharp fangs. These fangs are connected to a venom gland at the back of its head. As the snake bites its prey venom is squeezed through the fangs and into the prey.

Fangs replaced

Rattlesnakes shed their fangs every six to ten weeks. They always have at least three more pairs of replacement fangs lying behind the ones in use.

Forked tongue

The rattlesnake, like all snakes, uses its forked tongue to taste the air, ground or water. This helps it locate prey.

Dislocated jaw

Rattlesnakes are not able to bite or tear their food to pieces, so instead they swallow their prey whole. They do this by temporarily dislocating their lower jaws, which allows them to swallow animals much bigger than the normal size of their mouths. They will often take several days to digest a single meal.

A rattlesnake eating a rabbit

Factfile

More deadly snakes

Around 400 snake species have venomous bites. Luckily for us only a few of these would cause serious injuries to humans.

Black mamba

These fast-moving snakes can reach lengths of over four metres. They are very aggressive and will strike at a moment's notice.

Indian cobra

The Indian cobra is a very venomous snake. To make it look bigger it spreads its ribs out to form a large hood around its head.

Inland taipan

Australia's inland taipan is thought to be the world's most venomous snake. It injects venom deep into its prey through its fangs.

An Arizona blacktail showing its rattle

Rattle tail

Rattlesnakes use their rattles to distract prey and to warn off predators who may attack them. Each segment of the rattle is made from old, dry skin that does not shed. As the snake becomes older the rattle becomes longer. When the snake vibrates its tail the rattles bounce off each other to create a distinctive sound.

Super sense

Rattlesnakes can see with normal eyesight but they also have the advantage of seeing heat images. They use a heat-sensing organ to detect warmth from animals nearby. These heat images are then combined with visual ones in the snake's brain.

Rattlesnakes can see heat images

Scorpion

Scorpions have **eight** legs, which makes them part of the arachnid group of animals, which includes **spiders**, mites and ticks. Most scorpions are **nocturnal**. They tend to spend most of the daytime hiding under rocks, in crevices or within **burrows**. **Scorpions** have large pincers at the font of their body and a long tail that contains **venomous** glands. These tiny but lethal **predators** use their pincers to grasp prey and the sting in their tail to **paralyse** it. They mostly prey upon insects and small animals, but will eat each other if there is not enough **food** around.

Facts and figures

Scientific name Scorpiones	**Group name** Nest
Type Arachnid	**Habitat** Found in virtually every habitat
Size Head to tail from 9 to 20 centimetres	**Range** All over the world, with the exception of Antarctica
Weight Up to 60 grammes	
Life span in the wild Up to 8 years	**Diet** Insects and even other scorpions
Average speed Up to 6 km per hour	**Meal size** Up to 4 grammes

Sensing vibrations

Although they have up to 12 eyes scorpions do not have good eyesight. They rely on sensing vibrations through the ground to understand what is happening around them.

An adult buthus scorpion on a fallen tree trunk

Killer sting

There are over 2,000 species of scorpions. Only 40 of these have venom strong enough to kill a human.

Did you know?

Scorpions glow under ultraviolet lights. They turn a blue-green colour. Biologists are unsure why this happens. It could be so they can find each other more easily at night.

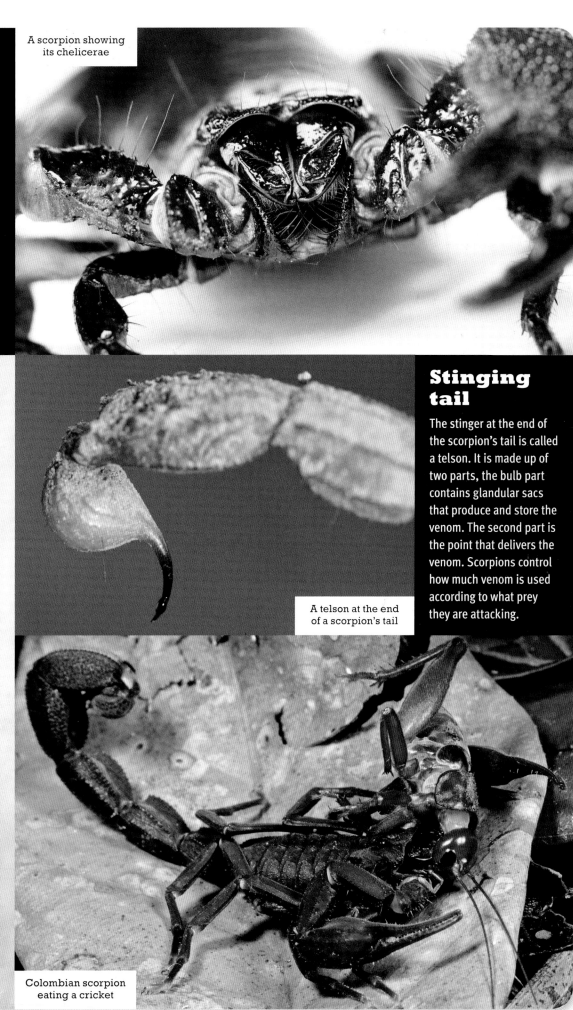

Built to survive

Scorpions have been on Earth for millions of years. They are some of the toughest animals. When food is scarce a scorpion can lower its metabolic rate and survive on one insect for a whole year. Researchers have frozen scorpions overnight, only to find they can come back to life when thawed out.

Mashing jaw

Scorpions use their chelicerae to eat. These sharp, small claw-like structures extend from the scorpion's mouth and are used to pull parts off their prey. They can only digest food in a liquid form so they empty digestive juices on to the prey to liquify it. Then they are able to suck up the liquid.

A scorpion showing its chelicerae

Scorpions often take a day and a half to eat one insect.

Tiny cannibals

Scorpions will often eat other scorpions. Mothers sometimes even eat their own babies.

Ocean dwellers

Some ancient scorpion fossils have been discovered with gills. This indicates that they once lived in the ocean.

Stinging tail

The stinger at the end of the scorpion's tail is called a telson. It is made up of two parts, the bulb part contains glandular sacs that produce and store the venom. The second part is the point that delivers the venom. Scorpions control how much venom is used according to what prey they are attacking.

A telson at the end of a scorpion's tail

Colombian scorpion eating a cricket

Polar bear

Polar bears are the **largest** land predators and the biggest of all bears. They are found in the frozen **landscapes** of the Arctic, Alaska, Canada, **Russia**, Greenland and Norway. Their main source of food is seals. Polar bears will wait by a seal's **breathing** hole in the ice until the **seal** comes up for air. Polar bears have to be **patient** because the wait can be long, from a few hours to a few days. When the seal **emerges** the bear bites the head or body of the seal using its powerful jaws. The seal is then **flipped** on to the ice, where it will be eaten by the **hungry** bear.

Facts and figures

Scientific name Ursus maritimus	**Group name** Aurora
Type Mammal	**Habitat** Arctic region
Size Head to tail from 2.3 to 2.6 metres	**Range** The Arctic Ocean and its surrounding seas and land masses
Weight Up to 720 kg	**Diet** Seals, the carcasses of whales and walruses and occasionally people!
Life span in the wild Up to 30 years	
Running speed Up to 40 km per hour	**Meal size** Up to 75 kg

A male polar bear in the snow of the Arctic

Did you know?

You might think that a polar bear would have a bright pink tongue but it is actually dark blue and black! In fact, underneath the polar bear's white fur all of its skin is black!

A polar bear can run as fast as a horse over short distances, reaching speeds of 40 kilometres per hour.

Furry paws

Polar bears even have thick fur growing on the bottom of their paws. This fur protects the bear from the cold ice and also gives them extra grip so they don't slip.

The science

The meat from one seal can provide an adult polar bear with enough energy to last for up to eight days.

Powerful paws

A polar bear's wide paws are adapted for life in the freezing cold Arctic. The paws help to distribute their weight when on thin ice. The claws on each paw are thick, curved, sharp and strong. Each claw can measure more than 5 centimetres long. Polar bears are excellent swimmers and use their big front paws as paddles and their back legs as rudders to steer them in the right direction.

Heat saving

Polar bears have bodies designed for survival in the bitter environment of the Arctic. Their oblong-shaped heads with small ears help the bears to conserve as much body heat as possible.

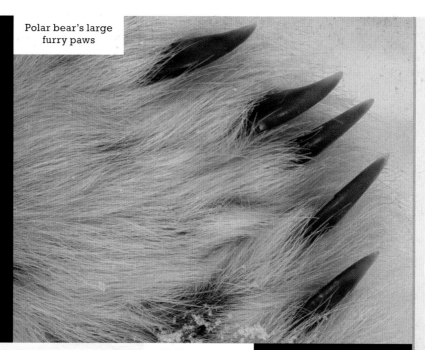

Polar bear's large furry paws

Mother and cub searching for food

Polar bear eating a seal

Amazing senses

A polar bear's sense of smell is so acute that it can smell a seal through metre-thick snow. These large bears can also detect scents carried on the wind from several kilometres away. The polar bear relies heavily on this amazing sense of smell to find food in the freezing cold winter months.

Factfile
More hunting bears

Most bears are omnivores, meaning they have a diet of plants, meat and fish. They survive on whatever food sources are available.

Grizzly bear

The huge grizzly bear survives on a mixed diet containing fruit, leaves and roots, as well as the meat and fish it hunts.

Black bear

The black bear hunts smaller animals than most bears. Its diet includes insects, fish and meat, such as deer fawns.

Sun bear

The sun bear eats small animals, including ants, termites, beetles and bee larvae. Birds, reptiles and turtles are also favourites.

Bengal tiger

Bengal tigers are the **largest** wild cats in the world. Their bodies are around 2 metres long and their **lengthy** tails add another metre. Their **beautiful** coats are yellow to light orange, with stripes ranging from dark brown to black. Despite **weighing** over 300 kilogrammes, these **heavily** muscled, powerful predators are built for **speed** and strength. The jaws of the tiger are extremely powerful and flexible, with large, strong **canine** teeth. A tiger's jaws are **muscular** enough to snap necks and **crunch** through bone.

Facts and figures

Scientific name Panthera tigris tigris	**Group name** Streak
Type Mammal	**Habitat** Forests, mangroves and grasslands
Size Head to tail from 2.1 to 2.7 metres	**Range** India, Bangladesh, Bhutan and Myanmar
Weight Up to 230 kg	**Diet** Moose, deer, pigs, cows, horses, buffalos and goats
Life span in the wild Up to 10 years	
Running speed Up to 55 km per hour	**Meal size** Up to 27 kg

A Bengal tiger growling and showing its massive teeth

A tiger's almighty roar can be heard as far as 3 kilometres away.

Tiger's diet

Tigers eat many animals. From small creatures, such as turtles and frogs, to larger prey like deer, antelope and bears.

Time to feast

Tigers eat until they are full. They will then cover the carcass with leaves and dirt. The tiger will return to it when it is hungry again and feed some more.

Did you know?

Unlike many other cat species, tigers are very strong swimmers and seem to enjoy the water. They often enter rivers and lakes to chase prey or just to cool themselves down.

Two adult tigers fighting

Puma

These secretive cats live in mountain forests where they hunt for rats, birds, fish and larger animals like sheep and raccoons.

Fighting cats

Tigers tend to avoid each other rather than fight. When tigers do fight between themselves, they rarely fight to the death, but they may recieve injuries that later cause death. Fights are most often caused when a tiger tries to defend, expand or acquire a territory.

Agile cat

Tigers have extremely flexible bodies that are designed for running, jumping and climbing. Their powerful limbs enable tigers to chase and capture prey quickly. The hind legs of the tiger are also longer than their front legs. This enables them to cover distances of up to 10 metres in a single leap.

Tigers use their tails for balance

Jaguar

The jaguar is the third biggest cat in the world. They live in thick, dense jungle and are always found close to water.

Powerful hunters

Like most cats, the tiger is an ambush hunter. This means that they lie in wait, before carefully creeping up on their prey, circling in as closely as possible and then suddenly charging at their target from behind. Once a tiger has caught its prey it locks its jaws round the animal's neck until it dies of strangulation.

Ocelot

The ocelot is a nocturnal animal that hunts at night. It survives on a diet of rabbits, birds, fish, crabs, lizards and snakes.

Tiger chasing sambar deers

Orca

The **huge** orca (or killer whale) is immediately recognizable by its distinctive **black-and-white** colouring. These creatures are sometimes called the **wolves** of the sea because they hunt in groups. Each group is called a **pod** and can be made up of up to 40 orcas. **Members** of the pod communicate with each other by using distinctive noises that they can **recognize** even at a distance. Working together they are able to catch a huge **variety** of prey, from large marine **mammals**, such as seals, sea lions, and even **whales**, to smaller animals like fish, squid and seabirds.

Baby orcas are born up to 2.5 metres long and weigh from 135 to 180 kilogrammes.

An orca breathing air at the surface of the ocean

Killer mouth

Orcas have about 45 sharp teeth. The teeth measure up to 10 centimetres long and are designed for ripping and tearing prey.

Huge range

Orcas have been seen in every ocean around the world. They are most common in Arctic and Antarctic waters.

Did you know?

Orcas sometimes raise their tails above the water and then slap them on the surface. This is called tail lobbing and is thought to be another way that orcas communicate.

A mother and her baby

Perfect parent

Female orcas give birth every three to ten years. The baby is born measuring around 2.5 metres long. A baby orca is called a calf. The mother orca will stay very close to the baby for for the first few years of its life. Studies have shown that all the members of the pod will help to raise a calf.

Coming ashore

Some orcas have taught themselves a clever trick to catch prey on land. The orca swims directly up on to the beach to grab a sea lion pup. The orca may get temporarily stuck in the shallow waters on the beach, but after a few minutes of thrashing it is able to make its way back into the ocean.

Inland orca

Very occasionally an orca will swim into a freshwater river. They have been known to swim for up to 160 kilometres inland.

Thick insulation

A thick layer of fat, or blubber, helps an orca stay warm even in the coldest of waters.

An orca moving on to the beach

Giant leaper

Orcas are often seen leaping, twisting in the air and then landing on their sides or backs. But it takes a huge amout of power and speed for an orca to leap out of the water like this. This pastime is called breaching and it is believed that orcas do this to relieve itches or simply for fun.

An orca breaching

Tarantula

Tarantulas are large spiders with a **fearsome** reputation, but while they have a **painful** bite, they are not a threat to humans. Though some of the bigger species of tarantulas will **hunt** for small **animals**, such as mice, frogs and even birds, most survive on a diet of insects. They hunt by very slowly **creeping** up and then **leaping** on their prey and biting them. Poisonous venom is pumped through the spider's hollow **fangs** and instantly begins to **liquefy** the the victim's insides. Then the spider sucks this liquid up through its **straw-like** mouth.

In the wild tarantulas can live to an age of over 30 years.

Did you know?

Goliath bird-eaters are the world's largest species of tarantula. As the name suggests it is large enough to eat a bird, although it mainly eats frogs, snakes, insects and bats.

The giant Brazilian whiteknee bird-eating tarantula

Hairy defence

The hairs on the body and legs of the tarantula irritate its predators. Some tarantulas will rub their backs to throw these hairs in the direction of the enemy.

Trip wires

Tarantulas do not use webs to trap their prey. But some spin a trip wire to alert them when something approaches their burrow.

A tarantula with a tree frog

Super fangs

The fangs are very important tools for the tarantula. Their primary function is to inject venom into the spider's prey, but the fangs are also used for grooming and cleaning the tarantula's legs.

Tiny mouth

The tarantula has a very small mouth and is unable to bite chunks of flesh from its prey. Instead it relies on several tools that help it eat. After it has killed its prey, the spider will start chewing with its tiny teeth. The spider salivates a liquid on to the prey that has dissolving properties. The prey becomes a watery blend that can easily be sucked up into the tarantula's mouth.

Factfile

More deadly spiders

Although few spiders pose any real threat to human life, these small creatures are fierce predators to many insects.

Huntsman spider

The huntsman is a large, long-legged spider. It has a flat body, which is useful for crawling into small hiding places.

Black widow spider

The unusual hourglass body shape of the black widow spider makes this venomous spider easy to identify.

A tarantula showing its fangs

A tarantula hawk with a tarantula

Tarantula killer

One of the very few enemies of the tarantula is the tarantula hawk. This wasp will sting the tarantula to paralyse it and then lay an egg on to the spider's body. After a week the wasp's egg hatches and the larva burrows down into the spider's body and slowly begins to eat the tarantula while it is still alive!

Wolf spider

The wolf spider is a robust and agile hunter. It has excellent eyesight. They are found in shrublands, woodland and forests.

African wild dog

The African wild dog lives in the **grasslands**, savannahs and open **woodlands** of eastern and southern Africa. Their long legs and powerful bodies enable them to run at great **speeds** when chasing prey. They live in large **social** groups called packs. They are one of Africa's most **successful** hunters. They work as a highly efficient team to chase, **attack** and kill their prey. These intelligent dogs **communicate** by touch, action and also by producing various vocal noises, including whines, **whimpers**, squeals and **high-pitched** bird-like sounds.

Facts and figures

Scientific name Lycaon pictus	**Group name** Pack
Type Mammal	**Habitat** From dense forest to open plains
Size Head to tail from 1.1 to 1.9 metres	**Range** Southern and east Africa
Weight Up to 37 kg	**Diet** Thomson's gazelle, impala, springbok and wildebeest calves
Life span in the wild Up to 11 years	
Running speed Up to 55 km per hour	**Meal size** Up to 5.9 kg

Did you know?

African wild dogs have very powerful jaw muscles. Their large sharp teeth allow them to tear through flesh. They can even crush through the bones of their prey.

A pack of African wild dogs after a successful hunt

The pups

The average litter size for the wild dog is between four and eight puppies. At three months old they are taught to hunt.

Caring families

The African wild dog will take care of the older, sick or disabled members of its pack. They will also look after the welfare of any orphaned pups they find.

African wild dogs eating their prey

Hunting pack

African wild dogs are cooperative hunters. They work as a team to chase and outrun prey, such as gazelles and other antelopes, baby wildebeest and warthogs. The dogs bite chunks out of their prey while it is still running; it will eventually fall to the ground and die from shock and loss of blood.

Killer pups

For the first 10 to 12 weeks of their lives the pups will stay around the den in which they were born. During this time whole pack works together to take care of the pups. After three months they are strong enough to leave the den and the older members of the pack will teach them how to hunt.

African wild dog pups

Wild population

There are between 2,000 and 5,000 of these dogs remaining in the wild, mostly in game reserves or national parks.

Huge litter

A litter of African wild dogs may be as big as 16 pups. Not all pups will survive to adulthood.

African wild dogs are among the most social members of the dog family.

African wild dogs attacking a hyena

Local rivalries

The African wild dog and spotted hyena share similar habitats, but they are far from friends. The hyena is twice the size and has a much more powerful bite than the wild dog, but this does not stop dogs from attacking them. Most conflicts happen because hyenas try to steal food from the wild dogs.

Komodo dragon

Komodo dragons are the biggest and **heaviest** lizards on Earth. These huge **creatures** have lived on Indonesia's Lesser Sundra Islands for millions of years. Komodo **dragons** hunt by waiting **patiently** for prey to pass. They use their powerful legs, sharp claws and serrated **shark-like** teeth to kill prey. These giant lizards are not fussy eaters. They are happy to **attack** deer, **water buffalo** and pigs, as well as feast on any dead animals they stumble upon. These ferocious **predators** have also been known to attack – and eat – **humans!**

Facts and figures

Scientific name Varanus komodoensis	**Group name** Lounge
Type Reptile	**Habitat** Savannah and forest near the shore
Size Head to tail from 2.6 to 3 metres	**Range** The Indonesian islands of Komodo, Gili Motang Rinca, Padar and Flores
Weight Up to 150 kg	
Life span in the wild Up to 30 years	**Diet** Deer, pigs, lizards and water buffalo
Running speed Up to 20 km per hour	**Meal size** Up to 120 kg

A Komodo dragon searching for prey

A Komodo dragon can **eat** as much as **80 per cent** of its **body weight** in one **meal.**

Huge appetite

The muscles in the Komodo dragon's jaws and throat are very flexible. This allows the lizard to swallow huge chunks of meat with great speed.

Sense of smell

Komodo dragons flick their forked tongues out of their mouths to smell their surroundings in the same way snakes do.

Did you know?

The Komodo dragon sees in colour as humans do. It is believed that these giant lizards have quite poor night vision, which may explain why they spend their nights in burrows.

A Komodo dragon eating its prey

Poisonous bite

The Komodo dragon produces poisonous venom like a snake. It will often bite its prey and then let the prey escape as the venom will kill the victim within a few days. The dragons then search for the dead body and feast on every piece of it. They will eat the flesh, bones, hoofs and even tough hide.

Komodo dragon's strong claw

Mighty claws

The Komodo dragon has long, sharp, curved claws on all of its feet. These claws are used as lethal weapons to kill their prey. They are also used for digging a sleeping burrow to rest in.

Attack mode

During the breeding season male Komodo dragons often have ferocious fights with each other. They rear up on to their back legs and do battle. The huge dragons attack each other savagely with their sharp claws, serrated teeth and large muscular tails. These fights can be very bloody and will continue until one of the dragons has been knocked to the ground.

Komodo dragon ready to fight

Grey wolf

Grey wolves are **slender**, powerfully built animals that are very successful hunters. They have long **athletic** legs that help them move swiftly. They live in groups called **packs**. Each pack has a **dominant** breeding pair, who act as pack leaders, and their pups. Grey wolves are social **creatures** who are affectionate towards each other. They communicate through sound, **scent** and body **language**. Grey wolves mostly hunt for large animals, such as moose, deer and **mountain** goats, but they will also eat smaller animals like **rabbits**.

A watchful grey wolf in the woodland

Facts and figures

Scientific name Canis lupus	**Group name** Pack
Type Mammal	**Habitat** All habitats except tropical forests and arid deserts
Size Head to tail from 1.2 to 2.1 metres	
Weight Up to 80 kg	**Range** Europe, Asia and North America
Life span in the wild Up to 8 years	**Diet** Large mammals, such as deer, elk and bison
Running speed Up to 70 km per hour	**Meal size** Up to 9 kg

Under threat

Grey wolves once roamed over North America, Europe and Asia, but were hunted to near extinction. The largest population now lives in Canada.

Close relatives

Grey wolves are members of the canine family, which also includes domestic dogs, foxes, jackals and coyotes. In fact all domestic dogs are descended from wolves.

Did you know?

One of the ways in which grey wolves communicate is by howling. A wolf's howl can carry up to 10 km through a forest and as much as 16 km across treeless land.

Pack hunters

Grey wolves have a highly organized social structure to allow maximum cooperation when hunting. The whole pack will work together to chase large herds of animals until one stumbles. When this happens the hungry wolves suround the fallen animal and swarm in to kill it.

Covering ground

Although grey wolves are able to sprint at impressive speeds of 70 kilometres per hour, they are also excellent long-distance runners. Packs of wolves will average 5 to 10 kilometres per hour. Packs of wolves will travel over huge distances while they follow migrating herds.

Grey wolves feasting on a deer

A wolf's **fear** of **humans** is so **strong** they will **avoid** rather than **confront** us.

Grey wolves can run for hours

Feeding the pups

Grey wolves carry chewed-up food in their stomachs. They regurgitate the food for the pups when they get back to the den.

Apex predators

Grey wolves are apex predators, so other than humans, few animals will prey upon them.

Vicious teeth

The wolf's large canine teeth can be up to 2.5 cm long. These teeth are extremely sharp, strong and slightly curved. This enables them to grasp their prey in their teeth and chew down through flesh and bone. They also help the wolf to eat nearly all of its prey, leaving very little waste.

A grey wolf's sharp teeth

Praying mantis

The name of these **unusual-looking** insects comes from the way that they hold their front legs, as if in **prayer**. There are over **2,000** species of mantis in the world. The praying mantis may be a tiny **predator** but it is built to kill. Their long, thin bodies have six legs, two antennae and a **triangular-shaped** head with **enormous** eyes. Most adult praying mantises have wings. **Females** are not usually able to fly, but males can. The mantis eats many insects, such as **crickets**, grasshoppers and ladybirds, as well as **frogs**, lizards and small birds.

Facts and figures

Scientific name Mantodea	**Group name** Swarm
Type Insect	**Habitat** Tropical and warm areas
Size Head to tail from 1.2 to 15 centimetres	**Range** Asia, Australia, Europe, North and South America and Africa
Weight Up to 10 grammes	**Diet** Moths, crickets, flies and other small insects
Life span in the wild Up to 1 year	
Running speed Up to 8 km per hour	**Meal size** Up to 4 grammes

Did you know?

Flower mantises are species of praying mantis that look like flowers. They attract insects who feed on pollen. When an insect gets close the flower mantis will attack.

A praying mantis kills a cricket by tearing its head off

One of the praying mantis's closest relatives is the cockroach.

Hot climates

Most species of praying mantis live in hot tropical areas of the world. Africa is home to over 880 species of mantis.

Eating time

Mantises will eat nearly anything they can capture. They often turn cannibalistic and eat each other. Sometimes a young mantis's first meal is one or more of its siblings!

Waiting game

The praying mantis is nearly invisible when on a leaf or stem. It uses this camouflage and waits patiently for an insect to crawl or fly by. As soon as this happens the mantis shoots its front legs out at high speed and grabs its unfortunate victim. This happens so fast that it is barely visible to our eyes.

Camouflaged against a plant

Amazing vision

As well as the large eyes on the side of a mantis's head there are three simple eyes between its antennae. Scientists believe the simple eyes tell the difference between light and dark while the large eyes see images and colours. Praying mantises are the only insect able to rotate their heads by 180 degrees. This gives them an amazing view of everything around them.

Clawed killer

Praying mantises are deadly ambush predators who use their front legs to lash out with lightning speed to grab prey. The spikes on their front legs help them to hold prey in a vice-like grip.

Huge eyes for all-round vision

Front legs hold on tightly to prey

Glossary

Ambush
The act of attacking by surprise after lying in wait.

Antennae
A pair of long feelers on an animal's head, which obtain information by touch, taste or smell.

Arachnid
A group of animals characterized by four pairs of segmented legs and a body that is divided into two regions.

Bask
To lie exposed to warmth and light, typically from the sun.

Bird
A warm-blooded egg-laying vertebrate characterized by feathers and forelimbs modified as wings.

Camouflage
Colouring that makes animals look like their surroundings.

Canine teeth
Special long, pointed teeth used for cutting through food.

Carcass
The body of a dead animal.

Carnivore
Animals that eat meat. Carnivorous animals often have sharp teeth and powerful jaws.

Claw
A long and sharp nail that an animal uses to scratch.

Dislocate
To put out of joint or out of position.

Dominant
The commanding animal of a pack or group.

Ecosystem
A group of organisms (animals and plants) and their environment.

Extinction
The death of a species.

Fangs
Long, sharp teeth that are used to seize and hold prey. Some are hollow and are used for injecting venom.

Fish
A cold-blooded aquatic vertebrate, characteristically having fins, gills, and a streamlined body.

Food chain
The sequence of who eats whom in a biological community.

Fossil
A remnant, impression, or trace of a plant or animal from a past geological age, usually found in rock.

Habitat
The place where an animal or plant naturally lives and grows.

Herd
A number of animals of one species that roam together.

Hibernate
To sleep, without waking or feeding, during cold weather.

Howl
To make a long, loud sad-sounding cry.

Insect
A small animal that has six legs and generally one or two pairs of wings.

Larva
A young animal that looks completely different from its parents.

Limb
A body part, such as an arm, leg or wing.

Liquefy
To reduce something to liquid.

Mammal
A warm-blooded vertebrate that suckles it's young with milk and has a single bone in its bottom jaw.

Mangroves
Flowering shrubs and trees tolerant of saltwater, found on tropical coasts and estuaries.

Nocturnal
An animal that is active mainly at night and which sleeps during the day.

Paw
The foot of a four-footed animal that has claws.

Plains
An area of land that is flat or gently rolling.

Prairie
An extensive plain of land covered mainly by grass, which in its natural state has deep, fertile soil.

Predator
An animal that hunts and kills other animals for food.

Prey
An animal that is caught and eaten by another animal.

Reptile
One of about 6,000 species of animals that breathe air, are cold-blooded and have scaly bodies.

Savannah
A warm or hot grassland area with scattered trees.

Skeleton
The set of bones, rods, shells or other stiff substance that supports an animal's body.

Stalk
To creep up on prey.

Talons
The sharp claws of birds of prey.

Territory
The area of land where an animal lives.

Venom
A poisonous secretion of an animal, which is usually injected through biting or stinging.

Index